The Science and Technology of TRACK & FIELD

The **Science** and
Technology of
Sports

The **Science** and **Technology** of **TRACK & FIELD**

Don Nardo

San Diego, CA

© 2020 ReferencePoint Press, Inc.
Printed in the United States

For more information, contact:
ReferencePoint Press, Inc.
PO Box 27779
San Diego, CA 92198
www.ReferencePointPress.com

LIBRARY OF CONGRESS CATALOGING-IN-PUBLICATION DATA

Name: Nardo, Don, 1947– author.
Title: The Science and Technology of Track & Field by Don Nardo.
Description: San Diego, CA: ReferencePoint Press, Inc., 2020. | Series: The
    Science and Technology of Sports | Audience: Grade 9 to 12. | Includes
    bibliographical references and index.
Identifiers: LCCN 2018052678 (print) | LCCN 2018052985 (ebook) | ISBN
    9781682826584 (eBook) | ISBN 9781682826577 (hardback)
Subjects: LCSH: Track and field—Physiological aspects—Juvenile literature.
Classification: LCC RC1220.T73 (ebook) | LCC RC1220.T73 N37 2020 (print) |
    DDC 612/.044—dc23
LC record available at https://lccn.loc.gov/2018052678

CONTENTS

Understanding Plus Hard Work Equals Success

A sudden hush fell over the huge crowd packed into a stadium in Berlin, Germany, on an August day in 2009. At the height of the world track and field championships, the 100-meter dash was about to begin, and the spectators had caught sight of the great Jamaican runner Usain Bolt as he walked toward the starting blocks. A tall, muscular individual, he had accumulated numerous records in the early 2000s. These include being the first person ever to break world records in both the 100-meter and 200-meter dashes in the same Olympics (the 2008 games in Beijing, China).

Many members of the crowd in the Berlin stadium had come specifically to see Bolt try to break his own world record. He did not disappoint them. When the starting gun sounded, he burst out of the starting blocks in an unbelievable explosion of energy and speed. Sure enough, as the fans roared their approval, he shattered the old record, running the 100-meter dash in an amazing 9.58 seconds. The vast majority of those spectators had no idea what physical laws and mechanical principles had allowed Bolt to run so fast. All they knew was that they had been fortunate enough to see track and field history made by one of the greatest athletes of the modern era.

Different Body Types

The crowd that witnessed Bolt's performance that day included people from dozens of different countries. Indeed, ever since the advent of the first modern Summer Olympic Games in

1896, in Athens, Greece, track and field has been one of the most popular sports in the world. Yet to call it "a" sport is a bit of a misnomer. That is because it is technically not a single sport; rather, it consists of three separate categories of sports combined into one venue, place, or setting at a given time.

The first of the three sports is running. Several running events, including short-range sprints, mid-range runs, hurdles, and long-distance jogs, together make up the "track" section of track and field. The two other sports in question together constitute the "field" section of track and field. One is a group of jumping events,

Jamaican track star Usain Bolt sprints to victory in the 100-meter dash at the World Athletics Championships in August 2009. Though thrilled with his performance, most spectators did not realize the various biomechanical principles that make such running happen.

including the high jump, long jump, and pole vault. The other features throwing events, in which athletes toss various objects as far as they can. The most familiar of these are the shot put, discus throw, and javelin throw.

What makes the running, jumping, and throwing events distinct from one another as sports is that the physical abilities and actions required to perform them are often very different. In a single simple example, a shot-putter or discus thrower needs larger-than-normal upper body muscles to achieve success. In contrast, runners and jumpers benefit more from leaner bodies in which the leg muscles predominate. Runners, jumpers, and throwers therefore tend to have markedly different body types and degrees of muscularity. In a 2016 study of track and field athletes, University of South Carolina scientist Katie R. Hirsch and her colleagues stated, "Track and field has [a] wide variety of events that each require specialized training and emphasis on specific muscle groups. Success in certain events may favor different body types and body composition characteristics. . . . Sprinters are typically lean and muscular; distance runners are smaller with little body fat, while throwers have the greatest amount of body mass."[1]

Generating Physical Force

In addition to benefiting from a certain body type, each of the three general types of track and field sports is supported and driven by specific scientific concepts and principles. Modern experts call them biomechanical principles. Each of the three major categories of track and field events exploits and relies on a particular set of physical principles.

Sprinting is a clear example. There is a complex group of mechanical concepts at work when a person runs, whether on a track or somewhere else. Factors such as muscle

biomechanical principle
A physical law or concept that scientifically explains how a person or other living thing performs various actions

8

strength, stride length, air resistance, and ground reaction (the ground pushing back against the runner's feet) combine to decide how fast someone runs. Sometimes the sprinter's leg muscles and strength are the chief biomechanical factors involved. Experts often emphasize those factors when talking about Usain Bolt. Science writer and reporter Liam McHugh points out that Bolt has more muscle mass in his legs "than other sprinters and needs more strength—more force—to move his body. With each step, Bolt generates enormous force against the ground. The ground applies that force back, propelling Bolt forward. Bolt moves more mass than other runners and he moves it faster."[2]

Each track and field event and performance is also affected by the kind and quality of the equipment involved. The types of playing surfaces and other physical factors also play their parts. Coaches and other experts are well aware of these factors and the many biomechanical concepts involved in the sport and frequently demand that their athletes learn about them. In this view, understanding how one's chosen sport works is essential to success. Former Yale University track and field coach Frank Ryan explains, saying that "hard work alone will not pay off. In fact, an athlete who works hard [without] understanding the [science behind] the event will actually get worse during a season. [A track and field event] will yield satisfaction and achievement only to those who understand it. Comprehension and hard work make for the ideal combination."[3]

CHAPTER ONE

The Running Events

"When broken down in its simplest form," says track coach and exercise scientist Steve Magness, "running is nothing but a series of connected spring-like hops and bounds."[4] During those hops and bounds, he explains, several physical processes occur simultaneously. The runner's heart beats faster, thereby increasing heart and pulse rates, and he or she breathes harder in an effort to take in more oxygen. The latter is badly needed at that moment by the muscles, tendons, and ligaments, which are taxed to a much higher degree than they are when the person is sitting or walking. The muscles push and pull at the runner's legs and feet, and the feet pound into the track's surface, as his or her arms swing back and forth to help drive the forward motion.

All of this physical activity generates a lot of kinetic energy, the energy of motion or work. "This energy," Magness continues, "is utilized and released, contributing to forward propulsion." It provides "the necessary force" required "to power the running movement. In simple terms, a runner can keep going at the same pace as long as he can produce the necessary kinetic energy."[5]

Standard Track and Field Footraces

Running can happen in all sorts of circumstances, some of them having nothing to do with competition, from hurrying to catch a train to escaping from an attacker. The running events, or footraces, in track and field are arguably the most formalized, widely witnessed, and exciting instances of human running. The specific events can vary a little from one sports venue to another. But most track and field competitions consist of roughly ten standard running events. They include several sprints, the most familiar of which are the 100 meter, 200 meter, and 400 meter. There are also some middle- and long-distance runs, among them the 1500 meter (almost a mile) and the marathon, which is 26 miles (42 km) long. (Contrary to popular belief, the marathon was not part of the ancient Olympics, but rather was introduced in the 1896 Athens Games.)

Linear Motion and Acceleration

All of these footraces have certain biomechanical principles in common. One of the more basic is that they involve what scientists call linear motion. Also referred to as translation, linear motion consists of a body traveling along a straight or curved line. Take the example of a car traveling on a highway. Every part of the vehicle, including the driver, moves in the same direction for a certain distance and in a set amount of time.

linear motion
The motion of a body traveling along a straight or curved line, as in the case of a car driving on a highway

No runner exhibits pure, or perfect, linear motion, since his or her body bends forward or backward slightly during the race. Those bends are an example of rotary motion, which is curved movement around an axis, or central imaginary pole. Yet compared to the runner's linear motion, his or her rotary motion is very minor; so runners employ mostly linear motion.

As the runner moves down the track, he or she achieves a certain velocity, or speed. However, almost always that velocity is an *average* speed, because first the person begins the race at zero velocity and increases speed during the next several seconds. Also, throughout the run the person either slows down or speeds up very slightly every few seconds. This fact brings the mechanical concept of acceleration, the rate of change in velocity, into the

The Sprinter's Start

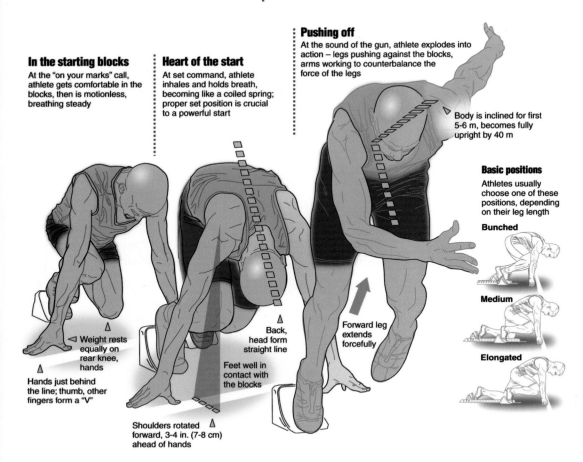

In the starting blocks

At the "on your marks" call, athlete gets comfortable in the blocks, then is motionless, breathing steady

Heart of the start

At set command, athlete inhales and holds breath, becoming like a coiled spring; proper set position is crucial to a powerful start

Pushing off

At the sound of the gun, athlete explodes into action – legs pushing against the blocks, arms working to counterbalance the force of the legs

Body is inclined for first 5-6 m, becomes fully upright by 40 m

Basic positions

Athletes usually choose one of these positions, depending on their leg length

Bunched

Medium

Elongated

◁ Weight rests equally on rear knee, hands

Hands just behind the line; thumb, other fingers form a "V"

Shoulders rotated forward, 3-4 in. (7-8 cm) ahead of hands

Feet well in contact with the blocks

Back, head form straight line

Forward leg extends forcefully

picture. At various moments in time, the runner either accelerates (speeds up) or decelerates (slows down).

Track and field coach and expert on biomechanics Tom Ecker tells how these factors affect a given sprinting performance:

> In sprint starting, because the sprinter is accelerating from zero velocity, the positive change in velocity with the first stride is especially great and thus produces the greatest acceleration. There is still acceleration with the second stride from the blocks since the sprinter continues to move faster, but the increase in velocity is not as great as with the first stride. In other words, while velocity is increasing with each stride, the acceleration is decreasing. The sprinter

continues to accelerate until the legs can no longer move faster than the ground is moving beneath the feet (usually the limit is about six seconds). Then, a steady velocity is maintained briefly before a gradual deceleration begins.[6]

The fact that a runner accelerates the most in his or her first couple of strides explains why a sprinter like Usain Bolt appears to literally explode out of the blocks. Technicians from the International Association of Athletics Federations (IAAF) carefully studied

Sprinters' Effective Striding Technique

Joseph L. Rogers, head track coach for Ball State University, here lists the various postures and movements involved in proper sprinting form. Each is supported by one or more biomechanical principles, including velocity, acceleration, air resistance, and ground reaction.

1. A foot that is moving backward under the body upon landing.
2. High heel recovery as the drive foot leaves the ground.
3. A support foot landing that touches down as close as possible to a point under the center of mass.
4. The ankle of the forward swinging leg should cross the support leg above the knee.
5. A very tall posture with a slight forward lean from the ground, not from the waist.
6. Arms that swing backward, as if reaching for the hip pocket.
7. Arms bent at the elbows.
8. Relaxed hands.
9. Arms that swing forward to a chin-high position into the midline of the torso but do not cross the midline.
10. Relaxed shoulders, neck, jaw, and face.
11. A dorsally flexed (toe-up) ankle joint just prior to the foot landing.
12. Head is erect and eyes are focused on the finish line.
13. Sprinter runs in a straight line throughout the race with very small amount of lateral [sideways] movement.

Joseph L. Rogers, *USA Track and Field Coaching Manual*. Champaign, IL: Human Kinetics, 2000, pp. 37–38.

this explosive motion. Employing a device that uses a laser beam to measure his position and speed every one-tenth of a second, they recorded how he accelerated from 0 to more than 20 miles per hour (32 kph) in less than two seconds. They estimated that the energy Bolt expended in that brief interval could power a smartphone for six hours.

Air Resistance, Gravity, and Arm Swing

A sprinter's or other runner's linear motion and acceleration do not act in a vacuum. That is, other natural mechanical factors come into play and affect his or her performance on the track. One of these factors is air resistance. As most people realize, air is not simply empty space, but rather is made up of trillions of tiny molecules that are invisible to the eye. These particles press against a person's body and other objects, creating a phenomenon known as air pressure. That pressure exists even when someone is standing still, and it becomes more pronounced if that individual runs down a track. This is because his or her forward motion causes more air molecules than usual to pile up in front of the body.

This air pressure factor exists even when there is no wind. So if there is a wind approaching the runner from the front (a headwind), the air resistance is even stronger, and if there is a following wind pushing at his or her back (a tailwind), the air resistance is weaker. To counteract stronger air pressure, whether or not wind is involved, runners tend to tilt their bodies forward slightly. This posture, called forward lean, makes the body a bit more streamlined and thereby better able to reduce the air pressure up front. According to Ecker, "When a sprinter faces a headwind, the increased air resistance requires a more acute forward lean in order to continue running in balance. And, of course, the headwind reduces the runner's horizontal velocity. Conversely, a following wind allows the sprinter to face reduced air resistance, which increases his horizontal velocity."[7]

The tendency for air resistance to slow a runner down is called drag. (In effect, the air's force "drags" the runner's body backward.) Drag is far more potent a force than most people realize. The IAAF technicians who used a laser device to measure Bolt's acceleration also concisely recorded the effects of drag on his average 100-meter sprint. Surely, they reasoned beforehand, a runner as muscular and powerful as Bolt could expend enough energy to almost eliminate the effects of drag. But this assumption proved wrong. The test results showed that a full 92 percent of the energy Bolt expended in just over nine seconds on the track was absorbed—in a sense, canceled out—by drag.

drag
A force imposed by air that pushes on and slows down a moving body

Sprinters compete in the 200-meter run at the IAAF World Championships, held in Finland in July 2018. The photo captures the vigorous swings of their arms, an action that provides added lift, helping to raise their bodies upward in momentary defiance of gravity.

Moreover, at the same time that drag works to slow a runner down, another natural physical force—gravity—does the same thing, only in a different way. Gravity is the force that pulls all objects toward the earth's center. As a runner zooms down the track, with each stride he or she momentarily pulls the body upward off the ground. This lifting action is appropriately called lift. Gravity naturally counteracts lift, in a sense yanking the body back down until the runner takes the next stride, in which he or she once more generates some lift.

Closely related to the battle between lift and gravity are the biomechanical effects of a runner's arm swing, which provides an extra vertical, or upward, motion separate from that provided by the legs. As biomechanical researcher Seamus Kennedy explains, "The arms can play a role in providing lift. As running involves an airborne phase [when for a split second the entire body is off the ground], this contribution to lift is helpful. As speed increases, arm swing becomes more important and arm motion becomes more vigorous and animated."[8]

The Biomechanics of Stride

Some of the other biomechanical factors that affect a sprinter's performance are associated with his or her stride—the distance between the touchdown of one foot and the next touchdown of the opposite foot. Every person has a natural average stride when walking, a somewhat longer one when jogging, and an even longer one when running fast. At first glance it might seem that a good strategy for a sprinter is to increase his or her average stride, since simple logic suggests that would allow more ground to be covered in a given time period.

The reality is actually quite different, however. This is because of the mechanical effects imposed by ground reaction. In the words of Warren Doscher, author of the highly regarded book *The Art of Sprinting*, "The track applies a rearward braking force to the runner's foot that slows one's forward speed."[9] That braking force, Doscher goes on to explain, actually increases if the

How a Runner Recycles Energy

When an athlete runs a race, he or she uses both energy stored beforehand in the muscles and energy gained from ground reaction during the race. Moreover, the person can recycle, or reuse, some of the newly gained energy as he or she continues to run. Steve Magness, a noted expert on the biomechanics of running, explains how this works:

> When a runner's foot collides with the ground, energy is absorbed from the impact. That energy can either be recycled, utilized, or dissipate. Instead of wasting the energy, the body has a remarkable system that allows for us to reuse the energy in a similar way to a spring. In this case, the muscles and tendons function as the spring, compressing and storing energy when ground contact is made and subsequently rebounding and releasing it upon push off. This spring-like mechanism provides a large amount of the energy required for forward propulsion. The key is putting the body in proper position [so that one touches the track with the forefoot rather than the heel] to get the most elastic energy return with the least amount of energy dissipation.

Steve Magness, *The Science of Running*. Origin, 2014, p. 22.

runner lengthens his or her stride. This means that any advantage gained by a longer stride is offset, or canceled out, by the increase in ground reaction. Thus, Doscher goes on, "Increasing stride length by reaching further forward with the leg is not the way to increase forward speed. It slows the runner by increasing the braking action."[10]

Coaches therefore routinely explain to their runners that the best approach to gaining and maintaining speed during a sprint is not to increase stride length, but instead to combine increased leg-muscle strength with reduced ground action. That is, the runner first takes the time—weeks, or if necessary, months—to strengthen his or her leg muscles, giving them more potential explosive power; he or she also strives to make foot contact with the track as little as possible, largely by increasing the speed, rather than the length, of the strides. "Strive," Doscher, advises, to use "stronger, quicker takeoffs and reduced ground contact time, but keep the motion smooth."[11]

This approach of employing fast takeoffs and reduced ground contact time is especially effective for hurdles. In most track and field meets, hurdling events are those in which the runners dash down the track while leaping over obstacles that are set a fixed distance apart. The most common hurdling event is the 110-meter hurdles. Each leap that a hurdler makes requires an upward takeoff similar to that of a high jumper, although the jumps themselves are considerably lower. A hurdler takes three strides between each succeeding hurdle. These strides must be fairly short to allow enough distance for the next takeoff. Thus, longer individual strides are actually a detriment to

A female hurdler leaps over one of the several hurdles she must clear in her event. In contrast with ordinary sprinters, who concentrate all their energy into forward motion, hurdlers must conserve some energy for the upward motion necessary to clear those barriers.

hurdlers, since they would hinder the timing and effectiveness of the jumps they must make.

Two biomechanical principles that differ somewhat between ordinary sprinters and hurdlers are arm-pumping and knee-lifts. Both sprinters and hurdlers pump their arms and lift their knees during each stride. Yet, for example, ordinary sprinters move their arms very vigorously, hoping that it will help increase their speed. In contrast, such dynamic arm movements expend too much energy for a hurdler, who must save some of his or her energy for the intermittent jumps. Therefore, coaches advise hurdlers to make their arm-pumps smaller.

The hurdler also saves energy by slightly reducing the extent of the up-and-down motion of the bending knees while running. That is, the hurdler's knees should not rise as high in each stride as the knees of an ordinary sprinter. These small modifications allow hurdlers to pour more energy into the all-important leaps over the hurdles.

Endurance Running

Air resistance, stride length, and braking force are also factors in long-distance running, sometimes called endurance running, including the 1500-meter run and marathon. These types of events are nevertheless distinct in certain ways from shorter, more explosive sprints. Endurance runners move at a considerably more leisurely pace for much longer time spans than sprinters do. So some factors, among them velocity and acceleration, are generally not major issues for distance runners.

aerobic capacity
The body's ability to absorb and utilize oxygen

Far more important for these hardy athletes is the biomechanical concept of endurance, the body's ability to withstand stresses for extended periods. Key to endurance, Ecker points out, is a runner's "aerobic capacity—his body's ability to absorb oxygen." During a track performance, "oxygen is continuously taken into the body's cardiorespiratory [heart-lung] system, which delivers it to the muscles. As long as the pace is such that the oxygen supply is adequate, the runner continues to function on the aerobic (oxygen-dependent) system."[12]

It also follows that the more muscle mass a runner has, the more oxygen he or she needs to take in and process during a performance. This explains why very muscular athletes like Bolt specialize in sprinting rather than long-distance running. First, their expansive muscle mass gives them the explosive power that propels them speedily for a relatively short distance. Second, sprinters are actually running on the track for less than a minute and most often less than thirty seconds. So there is not enough time for the oxygen they inhale during the race to reach all their muscles. That means those muscles must already contain most of the energy expended during the sprint, and bigger muscles contain more stored energy than smaller ones.

In contrast, endurance runners have plenty of time to absorb new stores of oxygen during the course of a race. Because their muscle energy is constantly replenished, their muscles do not need to be massive; plus, carrying a smaller load of muscles over a long distance is less tiring than carrying a larger one. As a result, endurance runners tend to have physiques similar to that of the Kenyan runner Priscah Jeptoo, who won the women's division of the Boston Marathon in 2013. At a height of 5 feet 5 inches (165 cm) and a weight of only 108 pounds (49 kg), her leg and other muscles are long and thin. Although her body is unsuited for breaking records in the 100-meter sprint, it is perfect for becoming a champion marathoner. Likewise, although Bolt's physique would be a disadvantage in a marathon, it is ideal for setting new sprinting records. That is why winning a track meet is a team effort requiring athletes with diverse body types and talents.

CHAPTER TWO

The Jumping Events

In a typical track and field competition, even as the runners perform their events on the track, the opposing teams stage the jumping events in the "field"—the large grassy area enclosed by the track. With occasional exceptions, there are four standard field jumps, each of which involves several moves and biomechanical concepts quite different from those in the running events. The first of the jumps, the high jump, requires an athlete to approach a horizontal bar and to leap over it without dislodging it. The contestant who jumps the highest wins the event for his or her team.

The second jump, the long jump, used to be called the running broad jump. This is because the jumper runs at full speed up to a block of wood (called the board) and from there leaps forward as far as possible. The length of the jump is measured from the board to the place where the athlete's feet land in the sandpit that serves as the landing area.

The third field jump—the triple jump—is sometimes referred to as the hop, step, and jump. It starts out similarly to the long jump, since the athlete sprints toward the board. But on reaching that takeoff point, the triple jumper first does a hop, landing with the takeoff foot, then performs a skip in which he or she lands on the other foot. Finally, the jumper uses that second foot just planted to execute the takeoff for the third component of the event, a broad jump.

The last, and typically the most spectacular, of the four field jumps is the pole vault. The athlete runs at high speed toward a high horizontal bar while carrying a long pole and at a set point plants the pole's front end into the ground. Driven by the momentum achieved in the run-up, the pole bends and flips upward, carrying the vaulter with it, and he or she maneuvers the body in such a way that it will soar over the bar.

Basic Jumping Biomechanics

One biomechanical principle that operates similarly for all four jumping events is an athlete's creation of a lot of kinetic energy during the run-up. The faster he or she runs, the higher the velocity. Furthermore, the higher the velocity, the more kinetic energy is available to be converted into achieving either maximum vertical height (in the high jump and pole vault) or maximum horizontal distance (in the long jump and triple jump).

Another mechanical factor that affects jumpers, just as it does runners, is air resistance. Strong headwinds or tailwinds can be annoying and on occasion disastrous for both vertical and horizontal jumpers. According to Tom Ecker, "Headwinds tend to shorten run-up strides and tailwinds tend to lengthen them. Even the most experienced jumpers have trouble making step adjustments with consistency when the wind is blowing, particularly when there are occasional gusts."[13]

A third biomechanical concept that jumpers regularly must contend with is achieving proper stability and balance. Maintaining one's balance in such events depends on maintaining support for one's center of mass, sometimes called the center of gravity. This is an imaginary point at which all of an object's mass, or bulk, is considered to be concentrated. For a ball, for instance, which is a sphere, the center of mass lies at its center, from which all points on its surface are equidistant. Locating the center of mass in a human body, in comparison, is more complicated. This is partly because the body has an irregular shape. Also, the body's physical configuration, or arrange-

center of mass
An imaginary point at which all of an object's mass is seen to be concentrated

American pole-vaulter Stacy Dragila competes in the 2000 Olympic Games in Sydney, Australia. To clear the bar, a competitor in this highly difficult event must combine the spring provided by the flexible pole with the power of her or his own arm muscles.

ment, changes constantly as a person moves into different positions, causing the center of mass to change as well.

Most crucially, no matter what position an athlete's body may be in, to be balanced and stable there must be a base of support directly beneath the center of mass. "The bigger the base of support," biochemist Scott Coleman explains, "the easier it is to

The Name of the Game for Pole-Vaulters

The widely respected former track and field coach for Yale University, Frank Ryan, wrote several books about the sport's various events. In his volume on the pole vault, he calls that event "probably the most demanding and complex event in all of athletics." He explains that very basic to the pole vault, scientifically speaking, is the conversion of kinetic energy—the energy of moving bodies—into potential energy—the energy of bodies at rest. He goes on to give some familiar examples of this process and how it applies to the pole vault:

> The gasoline in the tank of your automobile represents potential energy. It is converted [to kinetic energy] to get the car to move. If you [roll] a ball bearing up an inclined plank, it [rolls] more and more slowly until it stops. By rolling it, you give it energy of motion (kinetic energy). By reaching a higher position, it exchanges its kinetic energy for height, or energy of position (potential energy). [Similarly, in the pole vault] as you convert kinetic energy (the energy of your run) into potential energy (your height in the air), everything you do must relate to making this conversion process more efficient. Obviously, the more energy you have to work with, the higher you will go. Getting height is the basic job. Height is the name of the game.

Frank Ryan, *Pole Vault*. New York: Viking, 1971, pp. 4, 11–12.

balance. For example, it is easier to balance when standing on two legs rather than one leg. The closer the center of mass is to the base of support, the easier it is to balance."[14]

In the long jump the support beneath the center of mass is usually the legs, and in the pole vault it might be the legs, arms, or pole, depending on which part of the jump one singles out. Maintaining balance is especially difficult in the triple jump because the jumper initially lands on one foot and then rapidly shifts to a landing on the other. If proper support is lacking on even one of those landings, the jumper will lose his or her balance and fall to one side, ruining the jump.

The Vertical Jumps

In addition to these basic biomechanical factors, each of the four jumps has its individual traits that exploit certain natural forces and laws of physics. This becomes clear in a brief examination of one of the vertical jumps—the high jump. Initially, in what jumpers call the approach, the athlete takes about eight to twelve strides, then accelerates his or her velocity from zero to as fast as possible. It has been shown that the higher the velocity attained, the more potential height the jumper can achieve.

No less important to the jump's effectiveness is the takeoff itself. Here, several mechanical factors work together, one of which involves a battle between velocity and gravity. As the jumper leaps upward, he or she aims toward a spot just above the bar, in hopes of clearing it without dislodging it. That leap never takes the jumper in a straight line upward, however, because gravity's mighty hand is ever present. The pull of gravity forces what would otherwise be a straight-line trajectory, or path, into a curve called a parabola.

parabola
In field jumping, an imaginary curved line or path formed by the interplay between forward velocity and gravity

At the same time, ground reaction plays a pivotal role in creating the jumper's upward lift. The more vigorously he or she plants the takeoff foot on the ground, the bigger the ground's countering force. "Top-level jumpers exert a force against the ground that is as much as four times their body weight,"[15] one expert observes. Key to exploiting ground reaction and achieving a lot of lift in the takeoff is the contribution made by specific muscle groups. The great Canadian high jumper Derek Drouin, who won the event in the 2016 Rio Olympics, later credited his leg muscles with making his jump of 7.8 feet (2.38 m) possible. In fact, Drouin said, most of the work that went into the winning jump happened when he was still on the ground. First, his upper leg muscles flexed, creating ground

In the IAAF Continental Cup meet in the Czech Republic in 2018, high jumper Levern Spencer takes third place in her event. Although the takeoff, seen here, is the key move in the high jump, arm and leg swings while in the air add extra lift.

reaction; a fraction of a second later, his lower leg muscles added a bit more power to the mix.

A jumper's ensuing in-air moves are nevertheless important, experts point out. University of Southern California physical education experts Jesse P. Mortensen and John M. Cooper describe these moves, saying that after the takeoff foot hits the ground,

> the straight lead leg is swung vigorously up toward a point above the crossbar if possible. [The] lead arm is swung up over the head to aid in the lift and in maintaining proper body position in the air. As the lead leg reaches its highest point, [it] should take the jumper to the top of the bar. The right shoulder and the head are then quickly dropped to accomplish the turn over the bar. The hip, knee, and foot of the trailing leg turn out in a relaxed manner to complete the turn around the bar.[16]

Torque

Because the jumper's body twists in a curving action just before and during the clearance of the bar, still another mechanical force is involved. Called torque, it is a twisting, or rotational action or force seen in all sorts of physical motions in nature and daily life. One of the more familiar examples is when a person loosens and tightens the lug nuts when changing a tire. He or she uses a wrench to turn a nut, creating the torque required to loosen or tighten the nut.

torque
A twisting force seen in all sorts of physical motions in nature and daily life

Another familiar example of torque helps explain why the amount of force needed to accomplish such a rotational action varies and depends on how far the person making the action is from the axis, or center, of rotation. The example in question is when someone opens a door. Usually a person pulls or pushes on the side of the door situated furthest from the hinges, which lie at the axis of rotation, and the door easily swings open. If the person pushes on the side that is closer to the hinges, however, opening the door is a much more difficult task because it requires a lot more force.

Thus, the closer someone is to the axis of rotation the more force is needed to produce torque.

Similarly, torque helps carry the high jumper over the bar in a major twisting motion. In this case, the axis of rotation, or center of the torque action, is the bar itself. Using the analogy of opening a door, the jumper knows that he or she has two possible approaches to the twisting movement that will make clearing the bar possible. One approach is to wait until the body is very close to and almost even with the bar and then suddenly twist, generating torque. As in the door-opening example, however, the jumper's close proximity to the axis of rotation will require that he or she expend a lot of energy to accomplish the twist. The second approach to generating the needed torque is therefore preferable. In it, the jumper begins to twist the body earlier, when it is further away from the bar. The circle he or she makes in the air is a good deal larger and thereby less effort is required to accomplish this crucial rotational move.

An almost identical display of torque occurs in the climax of the other vertical jump—the pole vault. Yet although the bar clearances in the two jumps are almost identical, the approach and takeoff in the pole vault are very different from those actions in the high jump. First and foremost, as the vaulter runs toward the crossbar, he or she carries a fiberglass pole measuring from 10 feet (3 m) to 17.4 feet (5.3 m), depending on the person's height.

Next, the vaulter swiftly changes the pole's position in preparation for planting its front end on the ground. This move is called the shift. The pole then bends, and the person's high velocity carries him or her upward into the takeoff. In Frank Ryan's words, "immediately after a full and driving takeoff, you rock back on the pole to establish position"[17] for the rapid rise into the air.

Most of the energy of the vault is now in the bent pole. But, Ryan continues, "as the pole straightens, the energy is being returned to the vaulter," who suddenly pushes hard on the pole, leaps over the bar, and releases the pole. "Then the arms are swung upward to bring them clear of the crossbar,"[18] Ryan explains. Having cleared the bar, the vaulter falls safely into a big cushion.

A Champion Triple Jumper

One of the finest triple jumpers the United States has ever produced—Keturah Orji—was born in Hoboken, New Jersey, on March 5, 1996. She has competed in both the long jump and triple jump. One of her finest performances in the triple jump took place at the 2018 USA Outdoor Track and Field Championships in Des Moines, Iowa. Just before beginning her takeoff for her winning jump, Orji clapped her hands above her head. She intended this to get the spectators excited, and it worked. They cheered her on as she made her swift, powerful run toward the takeoff board. To this day, even Orji is not sure how much this boost from her fans affected her performance. What is more certain is that, as attested by all who witnessed it, her jump was superb. The ground reaction created in her takeoff was more dynamic than normal; plus, she followed up with an explosive secondary kick. The overall result was a jump long enough to capture a new national record for the women's triple jump of 47.88 feet (14.59 m).

The Horizontal Jumps

The other two standard field jumps put an emphasis on horizontal forward motion rather than on attaining vertical height. As a result, a different set of physical strategies comes to the fore. In the long jump, for example, following the run-up the jumper actually wants to avoid achieving too much lift because the more upward motion there is, the shorter the horizontal distance he or she will be able to achieve.

Thus, the person executes the takeoff in such a way that the angle of lift into the air will never exceed 45 degrees. Indeed, Ecker remarks, "the angle is seldom above 25 degrees."[19] Keeping the takeoff at that relatively low angle ensures that most of the energy built up during the run-up will flow forward instead of upward.

Once the long jumper is in the air, gravity naturally begins to pull his or her body downward. To counteract that downward-aiming force, at least temporarily, the person employs the legs and arms, including kicking the free leg (the opposite of the

University of Georgia athlete Keturah Orji wins the women's long jump at the NCAA Outdoor Track and Field Championships in Eugene, Oregon, in 2018. She is careful not to achieve too much upward lift, which would hinder her all-important forward motion.

takeoff leg) forward as forcefully as possible. As track and field experts Ralph E. Steben and Sam Bell point out, "Swinging movements of the free leg and arms at takeoff, coordinated with the application of force to the continually outward-moving center of gravity of the body, reaches a crescendo [climax] near the end of the [jump]."[20]

This attempt to use leg kicks to offset gravity's pull was wonderfully illustrated in 2018 by University of Georgia jumper Keturah Orji, the first woman to hold eight American national field records. In her personal best long jump, accomplished in Knoxville, Tennessee, that year, she did her preparatory run and takeoff, as usual. Once in the air, she also kicked forward with her other leg, also as expected. But on that particular day, all of the biomechanical factors involved in the jump came together in her favor, and her secondary kick lifted her body several inches higher than even she had thought possible. That allowed her the advantage of being in the air longer, carrying her to the impressive distance of 22.3 feet (6.8 m), more than four times her height.

The legs and arms play similar roles in the triple jump. However, in this event the predominant biomechanical factor determining the jump's success is ground reaction. Some degree of ground reaction, of course, happens in the takeoff and helps propel the jumper forward during the first phase—the "hop." More crucial, however, is ground reaction in the second phase—the "step." By very forcefully planting the forward foot into the ground after the hop, the athlete obtains the maximum of counterforce from the ground; and that ensures the success of the third phase—the "jump."

If all three phases of the triple jump are successful, the jumper may win the event for his or her team. Moreover, that person may even set a new record. In turn, that inevitably instills in the jumper a tremendous positive feeling of achievement. Orji summed up that feeling well when, following one of her record-breaking jumps, she said, "There's not enough words I can think of to describe it!"[21]

CHAPTER THREE

The Throwing Events

The standard four throwing events in the vast majority of track and field competitions, including the Olympic Games, are the shot put, discus throw, javelin throw, and hammer throw. The shot consists of a heavy iron ball that the thrower, called a putter, unleashes in an effort to achieve as much distance as possible. Distance is also the chief aim of the other three throwing events. The discus thrower uses a complex spin to toss the discus, which, appropriately, is a circular, disk-shaped object made of metal, wood, and fiberglass. The javelin is essentially a metal or fiberglass spear that the thrower heaves after a long run-up. Finally, the hammer is an iron ball attached to a strong metal wire. The thrower undergoes a spectacular spin before sending the hammer flying.

Speed and Release

Although their origins differ, the four throwing events have some biomechanical principles in common. From a general standpoint, the most essential one is usually referred to as "speed and release." In simplest terms it means building up a lot of energy by moving very fast and releasing that energy in a single, mighty thrust. Tom Ecker explains, "A small percentage of increase in release speed will always bring about a greater percentage of increase in distance, if all of the other factors remain constant. For example, a 10 percent increase in speed of release in shot putting and discus throwing produces an increase of as much as 21 percent in distance."[22]

The energy built up and released by a thrower is kinetic because it involves a great deal of motion. In a sense, the quantity, or sum total, of that motion is called momentum. Thus, if a thrower manages to release an object at high velocity, the throw will have a lot of momentum. In turn, increased momentum translates directly into the thrown object traveling farther than it would if there were less momentum. In general, therefore, a thrower's body mass and the velocity of his or her movements generate momentum, and the amount of momentum dictates how far the thrown object travels.

These facts show that a thrower has to be more than simply strong to excel in one of the throwing events. He or she also must be agile and capable of accelerating from zero motion into a very fast spin, windup, or run-up, and then an energetic release, all in mere seconds. Otherwise, it will not be possible to create the quantity of velocity and momentum necessary for a winning throw. As former world record holder in the discus throw Jay Silvester puts it, "Successful throwers must be *quick* and powerful, capable of very rapid acceleration."[23]

Center of Mass and Energy Transference

Another general mechanical principle that all four field throws share combines energy and momentum with the thrower's center of mass. When the athlete is standing still, just prior to the windup or run-up, all of the energy is potential, or nonmoving, and surrounds his or her center of mass. The object to be thrown—sometimes called the implement—also has a center of mass. Moreover, because the implement is at rest in the thrower's hands, its energy is all potential, like that of the thrower.

The object for any throwers, regardless of which implement they will hurl, is to achieve a transference of center of mass and energy from themselves to the implement. This transmission of energy from person to object begins with the windup or run-up. Because the athlete is now moving, the energy is kinetic rather than potential. Also, the faster the thrower moves, the more momentum is built up. At the instant he or she delivers, or releases, the implement, the center of mass and accumulated energy suddenly transfer into the object. Silvester points out, "This efficient transfer of energy or force to the implement takes place not only at delivery, but also throughout the entire run-up. This means that the implement must be positioned carefully at different stages of the run-up to enable a successful transfer of force in the moments just before and at release."[24]

German discus thrower Robert Harting prepares for a mighty heave at the European Athletics Championships in Barcelona, Spain, in July 2010. His almost ballet-like twists, captured here, show that the event requires as much agility as it does strength.

Within a second or two following the release, the thrower's body returns to a resting state in which all energy is potential; but the implement is still soaring through the air, having absorbed a burst of energy from the athlete. The object does not return to its own state of rest until it strikes the ground. At that point, the energy moves out of the implement and into the ground. As it enters the soil, the energy transforms once again from a kinetic state into a potential state.

This series of energy transformations the thrown object undergoes demonstrates another crucial mechanical principle that lies at the heart not only of track and field events, but nearly all sports. Physicists call it the first law of thermodynamics, as well as the law of conservation of energy. Essentially, this natural rule states that all the energy that exists in a given situation (which scientists call an *isolated system*) remains the same. In other words, none of that energy can be either destroyed or decreased, or amplified or increased. Instead, the energy in question can only be transformed or transferred from one form or state of being to another. This is why the energy of a thrown discus does not simply disappear when that object hits the ground and stops; rather, that energy passes into the ground, which is able to absorb enormous amounts of energy.

Rotary Motion and Angle of Release

In addition, particularly important in the shot put, discus throw, and hammer throw is the mechanical principle of rotary motion, also called rotation and round action. It consists of turning in a circular motion around a central, invisible vertical line or pole, the axis. The axis always remains in a fixed position, while the athlete and implement spin around it. "Rotational movement is the key to fine throwing," Frank Ryan tells throwers he coaches. "This round action has to be understood, felt, practiced, and mastered. Developing a mental state for building up round power should occupy most of your attention during workouts."[25]

Hammer Throwers' Extensive Spin

Of the four track and field throws, the hammer throw has the most extensive and powerful spin leading up to the release. Some hammer throwers use three full rotations (compared to one and a half spins for a discus thrower), and other hammer throwers employ a full four spins. The choice between three and four spins is usually determined by the athlete's size and strength. The best of the larger, stronger hammer throwers are able to send the iron ball sailing out close to 300 feet (91.4 m) using only three spins. Somewhat smaller throwers tend to add the extra spin to make up for their lesser body mass and strength.

A hammer thrower performs in a circular platform the same diameter as that for shot-putters—7 feet (2.1 m). To heave the hammer, the athlete relies on the three or four spins to impart horizontal velocity to the hammer while both the person and implement move around the invisible axis at the platform's center. During the last of these incredibly fast rotations, the 16-pound (7.3 kg) hammer can feel like it weighs 700 pounds (318 kg). Just before the release, the thrower angles the wire and hammer upward to transfer much of the horizontal velocity into vertical velocity. He or she releases the implement ideally at an angle of at least 42 degrees; the closer to 45 degrees the person can achieve, the farther the object will go.

As is true of other physical aspects of the throwing events, rotary motion involves the mechanics of kinetic energy, or force. Here the circular or rotational force, often called torque, is accompanied by two other forces that consistently oppose, and in a sense balance, each other. One, called centripetal force, is the energy exerted by the spinning athlete on the implement, pulling it inward *toward* the spin's central axis; the other, centrifugal force, is the energy exerted by the moving implement, which pushes *away* from the axis. During the spin itself, the two battling forces

centripetal force

The energy exerted by one spinning object on another so that the first object pulls the second one inward toward the spin's central axis

strike a balance. But when the thrower releases the implement, centrifugal force wins
the battle and the object flies away, following
a straight-line path.

At the moment of release, the quantity of energy imparted to the implement is, of course, a
major factor in the distance achieved in the throw. Yet
no less important to the throw's success is another factor—the
angle of release. Scientists have long known that the optimum,
or most effective, angle for an object thrown by a human is a bit
less than 45 degrees.

The ideal release angle does vary somewhat, since it depends
on the technique and physical attributes of a given athlete. Nevertheless, experiments have shown that the optimum angle at release
for the shot put is between 37 and 38 degrees. That means that
more energy can be maintained at that angle than at smaller or larger angles. Similarly, the most effective angle of release for the discus
throw is between 32 and 37 degrees and for the javelin throw between 32 and 36 degrees. Each athlete learns to obtain the appropriate angle through trial and error and repetition over time.

Shot-Putting Techniques

That repetition can be particularly strenuous, even grueling, for
shot-putters because their implement—the shot—is a good deal
heavier than the discus or javelin. A standard shot is an iron ball
weighing 12 pounds (5.4 kg) in high school contests and 16
pounds (7.3 kg) in collegiate, national, and international competitions. The hammer weighs the same as the shot; but the close to
4-foot (1.2 m) wire attached to the hammer allows its thrower to
match a given putter's throw with somewhat less exertion.

The putter must operate within a circle 7 feet (2.1 m) in diameter. Even a slight touch of a foot or other body part outside
that circle is considered a foul and disqualifies the attempt. The
athlete starts by holding the shot beneath his or her chin, facing

the direction opposite than that of the throw. Technically speaking, the word *throw* is misleading when it comes to the shot. This is because the person actually pushes, rather than throws, the shot into the air.

Two standard throwing methods are employed in the shot put. Both are effective, and some putters prefer one, while others opt for the other. In the first method to be developed, the glide—introduced by noted shot-putter Parry O'Brien in the mid-twentieth century—the athlete bends at the waist over the bent right knee. When ready, he or she suddenly thrusts the left leg backward, in the process dragging the body and right foot across the circle. Meanwhile, the putter swivels the body upward and forward and pushes off with the still-bent right leg and foot. As the body arches upward, the right arm, still holding the shot under the chin, goes for the release. According to Ralph E. Steben and Sam

Polish shot-putter Konrad Bukowiecki places fourth in his event in a 2017 meet held in the Czech Republic. He employs the rotational, or "twist," method, which resembles the spin used by discus throwers.

The Discus Thrower's Psychological Challenge

Unlike throwing a baseball or kicking a soccer ball—acts in which good aim is crucial—in discus throwing the goals are achieving power and distance. "Mastering the discus throw can be regarded as a fascinating psychological challenge," states former Yale University track coach Frank Ryan, who also holds a degree in psychology.

> It's almost like learning a different way of thinking. You need a new and different perception of throwing an object—a very radical reversal of throwing habits. What makes acquiring the new perception of throwing so challenging is that the old habits are strongly ingrained. They have been built up during your entire lifetime. You may have started your throwing career by tossing your rattle out of your high chair and then gone on to throw rocks, sticks, baseballs, footballs, and so forth. Your total number of throws may have reached several hundred thousands. In nearly every throw the object was aimed, and for good reasons. Accuracy of throwing is important in most situations. Consider the interesting psychological challenge that the discus throw presents. After aiming objects for a lifetime, you are suddenly asked to reverse your throwing habits. In effect, you are asked to regard the throw as an indirect result—a by-product, really—of your development and use of twisting power. The new approach is to concentrate on round power and ignore the direction of the discus flight.

Frank Ryan, *Discus.* New York: Viking, 1973, pp. 3–4.

Bell, "As the shot put leaves the hand with a powerful final snap of the wrist and fingers, the power foot is just off the platform [and] the entire body is completely stretched, with both feet leaving the platform precisely after the instant of release, as if the putter were going to follow the trajectory of the shot."[26]

The second standard shot-putting technique—the rotational, or twist, method—became popular a couple decades after the glide. Instead of the putter moving 180 degrees, or half a circle, as in the glide, in the twist he or she undergoes a full 360-degree turn. In some ways it resembles the spin used by discus throwers.

Heaving the Discus

That discus thrower's spin is one of the most graceful and visually exciting athletic feats in all of sports. The platform, or throwing surface, for the discus closely resembles the one for the shot put except that it is slightly larger, at just over 8 feet (2.4 m) across. A skillful discus thrower uses as much of the circle as possible during the speedy spin, in which he or she turns 540 degrees— fully one and a half rotations—before releasing the saucer-shaped implement.

The thrower, like a shot-putter, starts out facing away from the direction of the throw. When ready, he or she begins turning to the left, allowing the right arm holding the discus to lag behind during the spin. The thrower first uses the left foot as an anchor, then switches to the right foot, and finally back to the left one again before the release. In each foot placement, ground reaction naturally comes into play, but especially in the third placement. That last instance of ground reaction imparts a powerful vertical force, as do both the leg and arm muscles.

The ideal exploitation of the mechanical forces involving the legs in the discus throw are well illustrated by the German thrower Christoph Harting's gold medal–winning toss at the 2016 Rio Olympics. As he began his spin at one end of the platform, he planted his left leg perfectly to allow him to rotate his body in a balanced manner toward the circle's other side. Then, in the spin's last phase, Harting jammed his left leg onto the concrete hard enough to create maximum ground reaction.

A discus thrower's spin contributes a horizontal centrifugal force to the ultimate heave. As Ecker puts it, the thrower imparts extensive "horizontal force to the discus around the body's vertical axis. Then, just before releasing, the vertical forces are added. The total effect of all the horizontal and vertical forces applied to the discus determines the angle of release and speed of release."[27] In the case of Harting's winning Olympic throw, strong ground reaction and a great deal of centrifugal force combined to produce an impressive throw of 224 feet (68.28 m).

The Whiplike Javelin Throw

In the javelin throw, in contrast, the required energy and momentum are created not by rotational moves but rather by a fast, forceful run-up. The athlete begins at rest, holding the javelin in a roughly horizontal position just above the shoulder of the throwing arm. Then he or she performs a run-up of eight to twelve steps (although a few throwers opt for a couple more steps).

When the person nears the throwing line, it is time to begin transferring the energy of the run-up into the implement itself. To accomplish this, the thrower executes a tricky maneuver in which the body turns slightly sideways and one foot crosses in front of the other. At this same instant, the throwing arm

The Javelin Throw

The javelin throw occurs in several phases, each of which requires specific steps and skills to achieve the ultimate goal of a long, strong throw. In the pre-delivery stride phase (pictured), the upper body aligns with the lower body and the athlete faces the direction of the planned throw. The alignment of the upper body with the hips provides stability. This in turn helps the athlete transfer momentum from the lower body to the upper body and ultimately to the javelin.

Source: "The Biomechanical Principles of a Javelin Throw," blog, June 16, 2015.
http://biomechanicsofjavelinthrow.blogspot.com.

stretches backward, preparing for the final step and release. According to one expert observer, "The final step, known as the *delivery step*, allows the thrower to transfer the momentum built from the run-up into the javelin. This is achieved in an action that moves from the center of the thrower's body to the end of the thrower's limbs. It is a whip-like transfer of energy from the hip to shoulder to elbow to javelin."[28]

In the javelin throw, as in the other track and field throws, learning about and understanding these intricate biomechanical principles often makes the difference between winning and losing. Champion German javelin thrower Thomas Röhler, who won the event in the 2016 Rio Olympics, emphasizes this reality, saying, "Biomechanics and javelin throwing technique are closely intertwined."[29] More so than most field athletes, Röhler has studied the biomechanics of his event in great detail. In practice sessions, he repeatedly works on his delivery step, concentrating on the goal of transferring as much momentum from his run-up as possible. All that study and hard work definitely paid off for him in his gold medal–winning performance. Confidently and proudly, he states, "Research and findings from the javelin biomechanics helped me to throw further!"[30]

delivery step
In the javelin throw, the thrower's final step, in which he or she transfers the momentum of the run-up into the javelin

CHAPTER FOUR

Playing Surfaces and Equipment

The biomechanics of track and field are on the one hand driven by fixed, uncontrollable physical principles contained within nature and the bodies of the athletes as they interact with forces such as gravity, torque, and air resistance. On the other hand, those biomechanics are often affected by outside, artificial factors very much under the athletes' control. Among others, these include the structure of the stadiums in which the contests take place; the composition of the surfaces of the track and field; the design of the shoes worn by the runners and other athletes; and the materials and designs of the equipment employed, including the poles used in the pole vault and the implements featured in the throwing events.

Modern Track and Field Surfaces

By far the most crucial factor in athletic performance in track and field events is the surface. In the early twentieth century, before the advent of the more advanced track surfaces in use today, most tracks were made of hard-packed dirt or some equivalent. Often they were not subtly contoured to keep rainwater from collecting, so they were sometimes a bit soggy. (Today's professional tracks have a tilt of somewhat less than 1 degree to ensure water runoff.) In general, a wet track is unfavorable to runners because with each step they must exert themselves more than they would on a dry track. The latter provides them with more ground reaction, which translates into more spring, or recoil, in their steps as they move along the track.

Although the track should be dry, it should also promote extra recoil in runners' steps beyond that supplied by natural ground reaction. To that end, those who design and build modern tracks usually employ three distinct layers. The first is a paved asphalt substrate, or lowest level, laid atop sand or gravel. Because the substrate is hard, it ensures a maximum amount of ground reaction. The second layer most often consists of solid, firm, but slightly resilient rubber about one-quarter inch (0.64 cm) thick.

Finally comes the top layer, composed of a more textured rubber, also roughly a quarter of an inch deep. One of the most recent advances in track creation is to apply the top layer by spraying on a mixture of liquid polyurethane and specialized rubber granules; when dry, it provides a durable, springy surface ideal for sprinters. Paul Steinbach, senior editor of *Athletic Business* magazine,

substrate

The lower level or layer of a modern track

This modern racetrack provides runners with a surface that will ensure optimum performance. It is designed to allow them to take advantage of as much ground reaction as possible, which gives them a good deal of spring, or recoil, in each stride.

reports that this flexible "performance layer" returns more energy to runners than materials used in the past, "and this translates into increased speed."[31]

The field section of a modern track and field facility has its own set of needs and standard designs and materials. Overall, the field features flat, well-manicured grass. But the more specialized, high-wear areas employ a wide range of materials. The approaches to the high jump, long jump, pole vault, and javelin throw, for example, are often constructed of layers of asphalt and rubber, like the track. The landing pits for the long and triple jumps contain deep layers of very fine sand, while the landing areas for the high jump and pole vault feature large, specially designed cushions to break the jumpers' falls. The circular platform for the shot put and hammer throw is most often composed of concrete.

Running Shoe Design

The composition of a track's surface is only one outside factor affecting the biomechanics of those who run on it. Another consists of the design of the shoes they wear. Track runners employ different kinds of track shoes for different running events. Sprinters and hurdlers, for instance, generally use shoes with small cleats, or spikes, protruding from the front parts of the soles. These barbs give them a little extra ground traction and thereby allow them to build up speed more quickly. At the same time, the heels of such shoes tend to be reinforced with soft materials. This makes it easier for the sprinters to withstand the hard landings they endure during their relatively few but vigorous and pounding strides.

Long-distance runners, in contrast, tend to wear shoes with wide soles and small built-in, rubber-lined air pockets. The pockets provide extra cushioning for the feet, which can otherwise become sore from running for much longer periods than sprinters do. This is especially true for marathoners, who go nonstop for just over 26 miles (42 km).

Running expert Warren Doscher offers general advice not only about proper running shoes but also about other feet-related

This photo captures the moment when a row of sprinters begin to push against the starting blocks in preparation for their first stride. The soles of their shoes feature small cleats that are designed to provide extra ground traction.

issues. Whether the athlete is a sprinter or a distance runner, he says, "the shoes must fit the feet snugly, but comfortably, with no chafing." Furthermore, the runner should keep a close eye out for wear and tear. "Is each spike tight and secure?" he asks. Also, "the soles of the shoes should be checked to determine if they have begun to [come] loose from the shoe, [and] the laces should be checked to see if they have begun to wear and weaken." Any of these problems can negatively affect the quality of a runner's performance. Similarly, "the toenails should be trimmed so that they cause no discomfort when snugly fitting shoes are laced up,"[32] says Doscher. Ultimately, the experts say, sore feet, whatever the cause, can subtly change a runner's stride and make various biomechanical principles work against, rather than for, him or her.

One world-class athlete who knows the importance of proper running shoes is champion Spanish long-distance runner Leire

Fernández. She often trains by running on mountain trails and finds that often even the best commercially made shoes hurt her feet. She learned to get around that problem by persuading the popular running shoe manufacturer Salomon to make unique versions of its product specifically for her. "I'm lucky enough to have access to the Salomon team's prototype and tailor-made shoes," she explains. "If I like a specific shoe they make, I can sometimes make ad-hoc requests to [the team] and they'll adjust it as needed."[33]

Choosing the Right Shot or Discus

Just as selecting and maintaining proper footwear can improve a track runner's performance, choosing the right implements can help throwers achieve more distance and pole-vaulters attain more height. One example that track and field coaches sometimes cite is selection of the most effective shot for the shot put. At first glance, it might seem that all iron balls of a given width and weight are alike. The reality, however, is that their surface qualities can vary somewhat, and a small variation can mean the difference between winning and losing. A shot with a rough surface is superior to one with a smooth surface. This is because a rough surface slightly reduces air resistance and drag, and thereby the object travels a little bit further.

The importance that even a little extra distance can make in the field throws is well illustrated by what occurred in the men's shot-put competition in the 1972 Summer Olympics in Munich, Germany. The United States had won that event in every Olympic Games since the 1930s. American shot-putter George Woods hoped to maintain that tradition. But he came up against Poland's Wladyslaw Komar. Woods and Komar employed the same throwing technique. But Komar managed to obtain slightly more ground reaction during his release than Woods did. The incredible result was that Komar won the gold medal with a heave of 69.5 feet, or 21.18 meters—a mere 1 centimeter more than Woods's throw of 21.17 meters.

In discus, by contrast, the most important factor is the distribution of weight. Scientists point out that weight distribution can influence the distance of a throw because it affects the object's inertia. Inertia is an object's resistance to any change in its speed or direction of motion. If someone threw a discus into the air and gravity did not exist, the object would continue moving in a straight line virtually forever if not slowed or stopped by some force or other factor. However, gravity *does* exist and pulls on the thrown discus, causing it to slow, fall, and stop. In this way, gravity overcomes the discus's inertia.

inertia
The tendency of an object to maintain its speed and direction of motion unless prevented by some outside force

The amount of inertia that exists within a given discus is determined by the distribution of mass within that object. Tom Ecker explains that

> if a great amount of mass is concentrated in the center of the discus, it has a low amount of inertia. If most of the mass is distributed around its outer edge, it has a high amount of inertia. [Moreover] because a hollow discus with the weight distributed to the outside has a higher amount of inertia than a "solid" discus, its spin continues for a longer time while in the air, allowing it to stay level, [and] since the hollow discus continues to spin in the air and does not "peel off" so soon, it sails farther before landing.[34]

Benefits of Bendable Poles

Most people, including avid track and field fans, are unaware of these differences in surface quality and weight distribution associated with the common throwing implements. This is not surprising, since those differences are slight and not apparent to fans' eyes. In contrast, the differences in the kinds of poles employed by the pole-vaulters are both major and plainly visible to all.

Even Fiberglass Can Break

Before modern pole-vaulters began using fiberglass poles, it was not uncommon to see the wooden or bamboo poles break. Fiberglass is both stronger and more flexible than either wood or bamboo, and therefore its introduction considerably reduced the occurrence of broken poles in the event. Nevertheless, even a fiberglass pole can break. This can happen if a flaw exists in its physical makeup or it wears out from overuse. One of the most harrowing examples of a fiberglass pole breaking happened during the Summer Olympics in London in 2012. Cuban vaulter Lazaro Borges clutched his pole, ready to begin his run-up. When he reached the takeoff point, he began to rise into the air, fully expecting the pole to bend and recoil, sending him flying over the bar to victory. Just as the pole bent, however, it snapped and shattered into three separate pieces. The snapping noise was loud enough to be heard all over the stadium, and the audience emitted a loud gasp. Fortunately for Borges, he landed safely, narrowly missing being impaled on the jagged end of one of the pole's remnants. He was allowed to jump again that day, but he did not jump high enough to earn a gold, silver, or bronze medal.

Vaulters, coaches, and fans alike can appreciate that the pole should be as light as possible. After all, the less it weighs, the easier it is to carry during the run-up, and in turn the faster the athlete can travel when approaching the takeoff point. Far more important to the height the vaulter achieves, however, is the pole's elasticity, or bendability. The more bendable it is, the higher the person can potentially jump.

elasticity
Bendability, or an object's ability to bend

When modern competitive pole vaulting developed in the late 1800s and early 1900s, the poles were initially made of wood. They served their purpose at the time but had a major drawback. Namely, they did not bend very much. So when a vaulter finished the run-up and took off into the air while holding the pole, his or her body retained most of the built-up kinetic energy from the approach. The athlete then tried to use that energy as best as possible to clear the bar. Eventually, the Japanese introduced bamboo poles, which gained widespread use. These had more bend in them but were still not nearly as elastic as the fiberglass poles that came into use in the mid- to late 1900s.

The advantage of using a fiberglass pole is that during its dramatic bending action, its elasticity allows it to absorb a majority of the vaulter's kinetic energy. In other words, most of the energy built up during the run-up transfers from the athlete into the bending pole. Then, within a mere second or so, as the pole straightens itself out, it transfers most of the energy back into the vaulter, a springing action that helps him or her make it up and over the bar. Science writer and editor Amanda Onion gives a more round-

The bendability of the pole used by pole vaulters is crucial to gaining height. The deep bend in vaulter Denys Yurchenko's fiberglass pole at a national meet in his native Ukraine in 2012 will suddenly straighten out, sending him flying over the bar.

Air Resistance and Javelin Design

The goal of the javelin throw is to achieve as much distance as possible. Scientists and designers who have studied the javelin and the event know that the longer the spear-like implement stays in the air, the further it will travel. Moreover, because air has mass and exerts drag on thrown objects, designers must address the mechanical factor of air resistance. Immediately following release, a javelin clearly moves point first upward and outward. Studies have shown that at this stage in the object's flight, air resistance on the point is very minimal. Indeed, most of the air resistance throughout the flight is on the javelin's tail section—that is, the section behind its center of mass. As the air continues to push on the tail section, gravity simultaneously tugs the object downward. This combination of physical forces causes the javelin to steadily rotate until its point aims downward and its tail is higher in the air than the point. Based on these realities, designers know that the wider the tail section, the more air resistance and drag come into play. In turn, the greater the air resistance and drag, the less time the object stays in the air and the shorter the throw will be. The most effective javelins, therefore, are the ones that have thinner tail sections while maintaining a proper balance between the front and tail sections.

ed description of the complex energy transfers associated with this event, culminating in the pole's bending. She uses the apt example of Stacy Dragila, winner of the women's pole-vault event in the 2000 Summer Olympics held in Sydney, Australia, and later winner of other pole-vaulting titles.

[As] Dragila prepares to jump, she has chemical potential energy stored from the food she has eaten. She then runs down the path, converting her chemical potential energy into speed—or kinetic energy. Once she plants the pole, it begins to bend, slowing down Dragila's kinetic energy and transferring it to elastic potential energy in the pole. As the pole lifts her upward, it returns the potential energy to Dragila in the form of gravitational potential energy. By the time she clears the bar, Dragila has just enough kinetic energy remaining to carry her past the bar. On her way down, the gravitational potential energy becomes kinetic again and is finally absorbed by the mat she hopefully lands on.[35]

Using the proper equipment in the field events is therefore just as important to throwers and jumpers as choosing the most appropriate shoes is to runners. Similarly, all the athletes on a track and field team benefit from competing in modern, up-to-date stadiums featuring well-designed and well-maintained surfaces and other facilities. All of these factors contribute to a meaningful and enjoyable sporting experience for both athletes and spectators.

CHAPTER FIVE

Injuries, Treatment, and Training

The natural biomechanical forces and other physical principles that allow track and field athletes to perform their events can sometimes be disrupted by sudden unexpected factors. In turn, those factors, which also operate under the laws of physics, can lead to various injuries. In August 2017 at the World Athletics Championships in London, England, the great Jamaican sprinter Usain Bolt suddenly collapsed in mid-race. It was a dramatic moment that brought many spectators to their feet. Most witnesses were unsure what had happened. The Jamaican team doctor Kevin Jones soon cleared up the mystery when he announced that Bolt had suffered a cramp in one of his hamstrings, three large muscles in the upper leg.

Cramps, sprains, and tears in various muscles are extremely common in the track and field events. Ralph E. Steben and Sam Bell explain, "When an athlete performs any movement that will forcibly stretch or violently contract a muscle, injury may occur either in the muscle itself, [or] at the attachment of the tendon with the bone. The latter injury, known as an avulsion, may be the result of either explosive activity or constant, chronic pulling."[36]

Whether the runner has suffered an avulsion, a pulled muscle, or some other injury, the race is now over for that person. Overcome by pain, he or she realizes that weeks or more of treatment and recovery lie

avulsion
An injury to a tendon, which attaches a muscle to a bone

ahead, *if* complete recovery is even possible. Jumpers and throwers can overstretch or otherwise injure muscles as well, not only in the legs but also in the arms, shoulders, and back. Often, such injuries result from an athlete's not having warmed up properly. Or a runner, jumper, or thrower might accidentally take a wrong step or lose his or her balance.

Common Running Injuries

Whatever the causes of such injuries, by far the most common ones for runners involve the muscles and tendons of the legs. Typical is an injured Achilles tendon, the tendon that connects the lower leg muscles to the heel. The injury can occur from a sudden, unexpected, and severe twist that happens in the midst of a sprint; or it can result from steady wear and tear to the heel over time. Either way, the standard treatment is to reduce the strain placed on the affected tendon. The runner usually refrains from running at top speed for a while, reduces training times by half or more for a few weeks, and allows at least three days per week with no exercise at all. Also helpful are the application of ice packs to the heel area a couple of times a day and undergoing mild physical therapy with a qualified trainer.

Shin splints are another common running injury. The term *shin splint* is a general description of pain and tenderness in and around a runner's shin—the tibia, or lower leg bone. Treatments vary. One common treatment is to apply heat periodically during the day through sitting in the warm, circulating waters of a whirlpool bath. Steben and Bell point out that some trainers advocate the use of "ice massage and heat in combination." The trainer, or athlete him- or herself, applies "heat before and ice massage after practice, followed by application of ice bags for two or three hours when the athlete is studying or watching TV."[37]

shin splint
A general term describing pain and tenderness in and around a runner's shin—the tibia, or lower leg bone

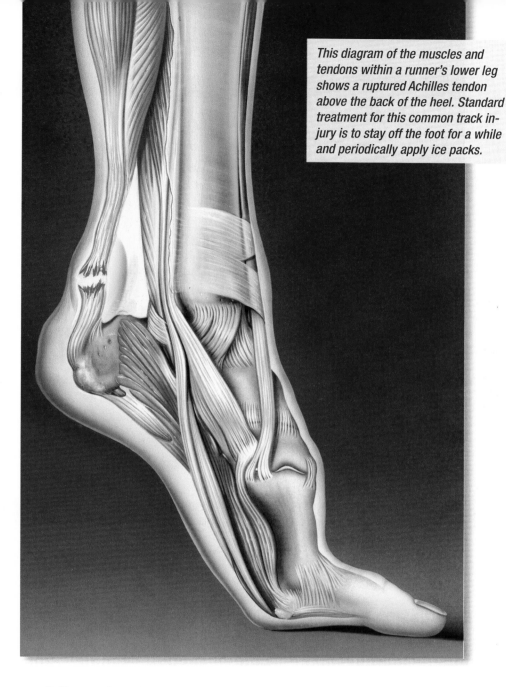

This diagram of the muscles and tendons within a runner's lower leg shows a ruptured Achilles tendon above the back of the heel. Standard treatment for this common track injury is to stay off the foot for a while and periodically apply ice packs.

Still another fairly frequent injury that runners, particularly sprinters, experience is a pulled hamstring. Located at the back of the thigh, the hamstrings are three muscles that, working together, allow a person to flex his or her lower leg. More times than not, the hamstrings pull when a sprinter explodes forward a bit too forcefully from the starting blocks.

Runners' Top Foot Complaint

Roughly 15 percent of all running injuries involve the feet. One of the more common ones—and in fact the one that runners tend to complain about more than any other injury—is plantar fasciitis. This consists of small tears or inflammation of the tendons and ligaments that run from the heel to the toes. According to award-winning science writer Christie Aschwanden:

> Runners with very high or very low arches are vulnerable [because] both foot types cause the plantar fascia to be stretched away from the heel bone. Other causes are extreme pronation (foot rolls inward excessively) or supination (foot rolls outward excessively) and increasing your mileage too quickly. Long periods of standing, especially on hard floors without supportive footwear, may exacerbate the problem.

> Plantar fasciitis can be extremely painful. The pain, Aschwanden points out, which "typically feels like a dull ache or bruise along your arch or on the bottom of your heel, is usually worse first thing in the morning." In addition, she says, the pain is most often worse after exercise, rather than during it.

Christie Aschwanden, "Stay Healthy by Avoiding These Big Body Breakdowns: How to Avoid and Recover from the Most Common Running Injuries," *Runner's World*, February 3, 2011. www.runnersworld.com.

Treatment for a pulled hamstring almost always begins with a protocol, or procedure, popularly known as RICE, which stands for rest, ice, compression, and elevation. For about twenty minutes every two hours, the athlete rests and applies ice to the affected leg, which is elevated and may bear a compression bandage. After a week or two, depending on the person, rehabilitation can begin. It consists of a series of stretching exercises designed to both aid in healing and strengthen the injured leg.

Jumping and Throwing Injuries

Long jumpers, triple jumpers, and high jumpers are no less susceptible to pulled hamstrings than sprinters are. This is because the forceful one-legged takeoff used by those jumpers closely resembles a sprinter's one-legged explosion from the starting blocks. Thus, it is not unusual to see injured jumpers undergoing RICE and following up with stretching exercises.

Knee injuries are also common among field jumpers, including torn muscles and/or ligaments surrounding the kneecap. The standard treatment for such knee injuries—providing they are not serious enough to require surgery—is to apply a protocol known as PRICE. It includes the four factors making up RICE and adds a fifth—protection. Here, protection most often consists of avoiding placing weight on the affected leg by employing aids such as a cane, crutches, a sling, or a brace. Over time, as the knee heals, weight on the leg is reintroduced a little at a time.

Both jumpers and throwers are unusually prone to pulls and tears of the muscles in the upper back. This is because the upper bodies of both of these types of athlete undergo strong and rapid twisting movements in the normal execution of their events. As with knee injuries, giving the back muscles plenty of rest is a must. Applying heat helps too, as do periodic massages done by a qualified physical therapist.

The throwers are also susceptible to injuries of the rotator cuff, the group of muscles and tendons that join the upper arm to the shoulder joint. In fact, a sprain or tear in the rotator cuff is the most common injury affecting field throwers. The injured athlete must immediately stop training and allow the shoulder to rest. Applying the PRICE protocol is highly recommended by doctors, who say that stretching exercises can begin after a week or two (depending on the seriousness of the injury). Over time, these can be supplemented by weight-bearing exercises and, hopefully, the eventual resumption of full shoulder capacity.

Another common kind of injury that afflicts field throwers involves the hand, including the fingers, thumb, and wrist. This is not surprising, considering that they grip their implements with their hands. Champion Australian female discus thrower Dani Stevens suffered a hand injury in 2016 during a practice session.

She told an interviewer that for a while her hand hurt so much that she could not do bench presses or other exercises integral to her training. Fortunately for her, she recovered and went on to win several competitions.

Warming Up

A number of the injuries suffered by throwers like Stevens, along with runners and jumpers in track and field, happen when one or more muscles unexpectedly stretch too far. As track coaches William J. Bowerman and William H. Freeman point out, "Lasting injuries may result from sudden stretching." For that reason, it is essential for all track and field athletes to undergo fairly extensive warm-ups just prior to competing in a meet. "A warm-up stretches the muscles, which helps prevent injury," the two coaches write. "All of the major muscle groups should be stretched. No sudden movements (such as bouncing or jerking) should be used, so the muscles are never strongly forced to stretch. The progress should

Two athletes warm up by doing stretches just prior to competing in a track meet. Doing preliminary warm-ups like these is essential in the sport because it stretches the various muscle groups, helping to reduce the incidence of injuries.

be gentle and gradual. Brief calisthenics may follow stretching. The athlete should be warm and sweating after the warm-up but not tired."[38]

Also, in a general sense, properly warming up before a performance can be thought of as the last step in an athlete's training—a lengthy, complex set of physical exercises and rituals that enhance both skill and conditioning. By repeatedly practicing the proper skills, or techniques, for his or her event, an athlete learns to exploit various biomechanical principles. For example, jumpers become skilled at certain moves that improve lift, which in turn counteracts the downward-pulling effect of gravity. Similarly, by learning how to spin and release properly, a discus thrower is able to transfer built-up rotational energy into the discus itself.

At the same time, amassing a lot of skill and conditioning reduces the chances of injury. So the regimens of training and warming up have the same overall goals—first, to compete without experiencing injury, and second, to perform well and hopefully attain victory. Hence, both regimens remain vital aspects of a track and field athlete's preparation for competition.

Flexibility and Endurance Training

Because track and field consists of three different kinds of sports—running, jumping, and throwing—the training program for each can differ in some ways from those of the others. Still, they all have some aspects in common, the most basic of which involves long-term steadiness and regularity. According to Bowerman and Freeman, "Ultimately, the most successful training program is the one that is most consistent. Athletes must train for weeks, months, and years at a consistent, moderate level. This stability creates a solid foundation for future success."[39]

One of the most fundamental and important steps in training for runners is achieving a good deal of flexibility. Track athletes whose muscles and joints are very flexible have somewhat longer and more powerful average strides than their less flexible colleagues. To develop good flexibility, a runner includes a lot of stretching in his or her training program. Another important aspect of training for runners is to increase endurance, the ability to keep going despite expending considerable energy. To a large degree, endurance depends on the amount of oxygen available for the body to use when performing a given physical activity. The aim of endurance training, therefore, is to ensure that the body can rapidly and efficiently take in and process oxygen as needed. The key to such training is aerobic exercises, types of exercise that increase the processing of oxygen, such as cross-training, which combines swimming, running, and cycling. In addition, some runners choose training programs specifically designed to increase endurance but with less-than-usual risk of injury. Realizing that many of her colleagues suffered injuries because they trained too hard, marathon runner Meghan Arbogast adopted a training regimen developed by Oregon track coach Warren Finke. For several months before running a marathon, Arbogast ran either full or half marathons in practice. However, on Finke's advice, she purposely ran them at 80 percent or less the pace she normally runs in actual competition. This method improved her endurance enough to allow her to win the Christchurch Marathon in New Zealand in her personal best time.

aerobic exercise
Exercise that increases the intake and processing of oxygen during vigorous physical activity

Strength Training

In track and field, athletes work to strengthen different parts of their bodies depending on their sport. As might be expected, for runners strength training concentrates mostly on the legs. The same is true of most jumpers (with the exception of pole-vaulters, whose upper bodies must also be exceptionally strong). In contrast, athletes who perform the throwing events concentrate their

Plyometric Training

Ball State University track coach Joseph L. Rogers is among the many modern track and field experts who advocate and use plyometric training for their athletes. In this passage from his well-known coaching manual, he offers some useful tips about plyometrics for both coaches and athletes.

As with other methods of training, it is important to know when to use plyometrics and how much to do. Jumping should start early in training. Specifically, in the second week of practice ground bounds need to start. For example, on Tuesdays and Fridays, have the athlete do the following four jumps five times each: double-leg forward; double-leg for height; single-leg standing forward for distance (five times each leg); and alternate leg bounds (10 total takeoffs). Increase the weight, time, or distance of the jumps as the athlete matures [gets more proficient]. This type of work should follow the intensity and volume protocol [procedure] used in the athlete's weight-training program. Change training loads throughout the season to shock the system. The body needs change every few weeks, and increases or reductions of load will help the athletes avoid becoming stale and unable to improve their speed development. It also improves the athletes' ability to adapt to different types, volumes, and intensities of training.

Joseph L. Rogers, *USA Track and Field Coaching Manual.* Champaign, IL: Human Kinetics, 2000, p. 43.

strength training on the muscles of the upper body, particularly the shoulders, arms, and upper back.

No matter which body parts one emphasizes, however, all strength training involves a biomechanical principle called resistance. A resistance exercise is one in which the muscles repeatedly pull, push, or lift heavy objects. During this activity, the muscles need to manage increasingly higher weight demands. So over the course of time, the fibers making up muscle tissue respond by growing tougher and at the same time stronger.

A number of approaches to resistance exercise exist, but by far the most common and popular one is weight training. One of the chief biomechanical principles of weight training is so-called progressive loading, which challenges the muscles to grow tougher by steadily increasing the amount of weight handled in a given exercise. This is most effectively and safely accomplished a little at a time, as Jay Silvester explains: "In any progressive loading program, it is important that resistance not be added too quickly, especially when working with young athletes. Adding resistance carefully is appropriate for anyone, but it is particularly relevant for the novice. Too much resistance or too many repetitions can result in injury and chronic joint problems."[40]

Muscle recovery is also a vital component of weight training. That is, in order to grow steadily stronger, the muscles must rest for a while before they are heavily challenged again. Thus, Bowerman and Freeman point out, "Resistance exercises are generally used three times a week, on alternating days to permit the muscles to recover." They explain that a sort of golden rule of weight training is that "no muscle group [should be] trained on consecutive days."[41]

Plyometric Training

An important variation of strength training emphasizes an aspect of athletic performance employed by runners, jumpers, and throwers alike. Namely, at one point or another all of them engage in some kind of sudden, explosive movement. For runners it is most often the initial forward lunge from the blocks; for jumpers it is their energetic takeoff; and for throwers it is the powerful release of the shot put or other implement.

The most common training approach used today to develop such explosive power is plyometric training, or plyometrics. It is also sometimes more simply referred to as "bounding." This is because the athlete often bounds, or jumps and hops, repeat-

edly, with each bound emphasizing a single outburst of explosive strength.

One kind of plyometric training has the person jump up onto a box or jump down from the box. This continues repeatedly, but with brief pauses between the jumps so that the muscles have a chance to relax. Variations include alternating single leg jumps with double leg jumps and changing the height of the boxes. Trainers advocate changing the routine at least every couple of weeks so that the body is constantly challenged to deal with a wide range of situations. That works a certain degree of flexibility training into explosive strength training.

In still another variation of strength training, champion discus thrower Dan John prefers a program that combines more familiar strength exercises with plyometric ones, but all done in a low-key workout repeated five times per week. He first warms up for five minutes or so. Then he does a weightlifting exercise while bending his hips. Next, he does a traditional bench press while lying on his back and follows that with some pull-ups on a bar and an exercise for his abdominal area. Finally, he performs some rapid jumping or some other kind of plyometric exercise.

plyometrics
A relatively new form of training that develops an athlete's ability to make sudden, explosive movements

Making Use of Video

Another aid to training that has been shown to benefit runners, jumpers, and throwers alike places zero stress on the muscles and other body parts. Instead, it utilizes a unique melding of biology and mechanics that was not possible before the late twentieth century. This merger of human and machine consists of video replays of athletes performing their events. Germany's champion javelin thrower Thomas Röhler, for example, strongly recommends this approach, saying that it gives him a "subjective feel for the individual relevant parameters of the javelin throwing technique."[42]

Renowned coach Frank Ryan agrees with the importance of the athlete gaining "a visual feel" for his or her event. "The event becomes clear in your mental imagery," he says. "You can run it in your mind like a motion picture film." Ryan also underlines that overall the most effective way to train is to combine this heightened visual sense with "muscle feel," which results from intense flexibility, endurance, and strength exercises. When combined, all of these approaches to training can help a dedicated athlete achieve ultimate victory. "Enjoy the challenge of mastering your event," he adds, along with "the excitement of competition, and the satisfaction of achievement."[43]

SOURCE NOTES

Introduction: Understanding Plus Hard Work Equals Success

1. Katie R. Hirsch et al., "Body Composition and Muscle Characteristics of Division I Track and Field Athletes," *Journal of Strength and Conditioning Research*, May 2016, p. 1232.
2. Liam McHugh, "The Biomechanics of Usain Bolt," *NBC Learn*, July 11, 2012. https://archives.nbclearn.com.
3. Frank Ryan, *Discus*. New York: Viking, 1973, p. 3.

Chapter One: The Running Events

4. Steve Magness, *The Science of Running*. Origin, 2014, p. 11.
5. Magness, *The Science of Running*, p. 11.
6. Tom Ecker, *Basic Track and Field Biomechanics*. Los Angeles: Tafnews, 1985, p. 16.
7. Ecker, *Basic Track and Field Biomechanics*, p. 18.
8. Seamus Kennedy, "The Biomechanics of Running," *O&P Edge*, March 2017. https://opedge.com.
9. Warren Doscher, *The Art of Sprinting*. London: McFarland, 2009, p. 92.
10. Doscher, *The Art of Sprinting*, pp. 92–93.
11. Doscher, *The Art of Sprinting*, p. 105.
12. Ecker, *Basic Track and Field Biomechanics*, p. 89.

Chapter Two: The Jumping Events

13. Ecker, *Basic Track and Field Biomechanics*, p. 19.
14. Scott Coleman, "Balance: The Most Important Aspect of Surfing," SurfScience, 2018. www.surfscience.com.
15. Ecker, *Basic Track and Field Biomechanics*, p. 115.

16. Jesse P. Mortensen and John M. Cooper, *Track and Field for Coach and Athlete*. Englewood Cliffs, NJ: Prentice Hall, 1970, p. 166.
17. Frank Ryan, *Pole Vault*. New York: Viking, 1971, p. 34.
18. Ryan, *Pole Vault*, pp. 36, 38.
19. Ecker, *Basic Track and Field Biomechanics*, p. 136.
20. Ralph E. Steben and Sam Bell, *Track and Field: An Administrative Approach to the Science of Coaching*. New York: Wiley, 1978, pp. 78–79.
21. Quoted in YouTube, *Katurah Orji Interview*, March 12, 2016. www.youtube.com/watch?v=7HpXCQ_uwyk.

Chapter Three: The Throwing Events

22. Tom Ecker et al., eds., *Olympic Track and Field Techniques: An Illustrated Guide to Developing Champions*. West Nyack, NY: Parker, 1974, pp. 178, 180.
23. Jay Silvester, ed., *The Complete Book of Throws*. Champaign, IL: Human Kinetics, 2003, p. 3.
24. Silvester, *The Complete Book of Throws*, p. 4.
25. Ryan, *Discus*, p. 39.
26. Steben and Bell, *Track and Field*, p. 140.
27. Ecker, *Basic Track and Field Biomechanics*, p. 172.
28. Conversation, "Science of the Spear: Biomechanics of a Javelin Throw," July 31, 2014. https://theconversation.com.
29. Thomas Röhler, "Javelin Biomechanics and Technique," Thomas Röhler, February 18, 2017. www.thomas-roehler.de.
30. Röhler, "Javelin Biomechanics and Technique."

Chapter Four: Playing Surfaces and Equipment

31. Paul Steinbach, "Surfacing the Modern Track and Field Facility," *Athletic Business*, September 2017. www.athleticbusiness.com.
32. Doscher, *The Art of Sprinting*, p. 47.

33. Quoted in Coty Levandoski, "These Pros' Fave Shoes Will Make You Want to Run," *Red Bull*, August 30, 2017. www .redbull.com.
34. Ecker et al., *Olympic Track and Field Techniques*, pp. 183–84.
35. Amanda Onion, "The Physics of Pole Vaulting," ABC News, August 18, 2018. https://abcnews.go.com.

Chapter Five: Injuries, Treatment, and Training

36. Steben and Bell, *Track and Field*, p. 315.
37. Steben and Bell, *Track and Field*, p. 313.
38. William J. Bowerman and William H. Freeman, *High-Performance Training for Track and Field*. Champaign, IL: Leisure, 1991, p. 13.
39. Bowerman and Freeman, *High-Performance Training for Track and Field*, p. 15.
40. Silvester, *The Complete Book of Throws*, p. 8.
41. Bowerman and Freeman, *High-Performance Training for Track and Field*, p. 11.
42. Röhler, "Javelin Biomechanics and Technique."
43. Ryan, *Discus*, p. 56.

FOR FURTHER RESEARCH

Books

Lisa J. Amstulz, *The Science Behind Track and Field*. North Mankato, MN: Capstone, 2016.

Gideon Ariel and Ann P. Ariel, *The Discus Thrower and His Dream Factory*. Pennsauken, NJ: Book Baby, 2017.

John Brewer, *Running Science*. Chicago: University of Chicago Press, 2018.

Peter Douglas, *Track and Field: Conditioning for Greatness*. Broomall, PA: Mason Crest, 2017.

Todd Kortemeier, *12 Reasons to Love Track and Field*. Mankato, MN: 12-Story Library, 2018.

Steve Magness, *The Science of Running*. Origin, 2014.

Internet Sources

Allison Campbell et al., "The Law of Conservation of Energy," 2018. https://energyeducation.ca/encyclopedia/Law_of_con servation_of_energy.

Scott Cappos, "Shot Put and Discus: Technique and Training," Digital Track and Field. http://digitaltrackandfield.com.

Conversation, "Science of the Spear: Biomechanics of a Javelin Throw," July 31, 2014. https://theconversation.com.

Iain Fletcher, "Biomechanical Principles in Sprint Running: Basic Concepts," Ariel Dynamics. www1.arielnet.com.

Peter M. McGinnis, "Mechanics of the Pole Vault," USA Track & Field. www.usatf.org.

MIT Technology Review, "Biomechanical Problem of Shot Putting Finally Solved," August 3, 2010. www.technologyreview.com.

Topend Sports, "Biomechanics and Lane Selection," 2008. www .topendsports.com.

Websites

Athletics Events, Topend Sports (www.topendsports.com/ sport/athletics/events.htm). Using the alternate name for track and field, athletics, this site presents links to overviews of all the events included in track and field competitions.

Track and Field History and the Origins of the Sport, Athnet (www.athleticscholarships.net/history-of-track-and-field.htm). In addition to the historical background of track and field, this site provides links to colleges and professional sports organizations that aid young athletes in joining some of America's finest track and field teams.

USA Track & Field (www.usatf.org). The home page of this well-known sports organization features links to all manner of information about the sport, including athlete biographies, current and past records in various events, the latest news about the sport, and more.

INDEX

PICTURE CREDITS

ABOUT THE AUTHOR

In addition to his numerous acclaimed volumes on ancient civilizations, historian Don Nardo has published several studies of scientific discoveries and phenomena, including *Deadliest Dinosaurs*, *Climate Change*, *Polar Explorations*, *Volcanoes*, *Science and Sustainable Energy*, and award-winning books on astronomy and space exploration. Nardo also composes and arranges orchestral music. He lives with his wife, Christine, in Massachusetts.